Letter from RCMP officer

Issues of personal safety and security continue to capture our attention as well as the headlines. I recommend that all teenagers give considerable thought to educating themselves in basic self-defense. This training could be one of the most valuable experiences of a teenager's life. Much like learning a language, self-defense techniques must be practiced to be performed without hesitation. Learning self-defense is more than blocks and punches; it's learning to be assertive and confident. It also builds self-esteem and promotes self-discipline.

Practice these techniques as part of your regular exercise program so that you may react quickly should the need arise.

The techniques Dr. Konzak teaches are intelligent, effective and surprisingly gentle. Whether choosing to practice alone, with a friend, with a parent or with a trained teacher, long-term practice is necessary in mastering techniques of self-defense. This book should serve as a useful practice guide for all teenagers who wish to learn self-defense on their own.

Parents have a responsibility to ensure the safety of their children. They can do this by making rules or leaving them with people they trust. At a young age, this is a manageable task; however, teenagers are exposed to a variety of dangers and risks of which parents are often not cognizant. Take the time to learn and practice these techniques with your children. Their knowledge of self-defense will give you the confidence that they will be able to defend themselves.

Constable David Hvidston
Royal Canadian Mounted Police

GIRL POWER

self-defense for teens

Written by
Burt Konzak, Ph.D.

With Assistance by
Sonya and Mélina Konzak

Designed by
Vivian Ducas

Sport Books Publisher

Sport Books Publisher

Design by Vivian Ducas
Cover by Urška Krašovic
Photography by Donna Maloney, Ganesh Murdeshwar

Canadian Cataloguing in Publication Data

Konzak, Burt, 1946-
Girl Power: self-defense for teens

Includes bibliographical references.
ISBN 0-920905-60-9

1. Self-defense for women. I. Konzak, Sonya. II. Konzak, Mélina. III. Title.

GV1111.5.K66 1999   613.6'6'08352   C99-930897-1

Summary: *A resource of self-defense understandings, inspirational proverbs, how to instructions, confrontation avoidance techniques, lists for help centres and organizations and more for teens, especially girls. Includes a separate helpful appendix for parents, guardians, and teachers.*

Distribution worldwide by Sport Books Publisher

http://www.sportbookspub.com
E-mail: sbp@sportbookspub.com
Fax: 416 966-9022

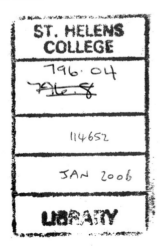

Acknowledgements

It was a great pleasure writing this book, and the pleasure of the company of the people who contributed their ideas and support made it all the more wonderful. I would like to express special acknowledgement:

To Vivian Ducas who contributed much more than just the design of this book; her ideas and enthusiasm were an invaluable part of this project.

To Gerhard Schmitt, author of *Mädchen Lernen Sich zu Wehren*,[5] his excellently written and thought-out book on self-defense for girls was an important contribution. Many of his ideas were incorporated into the book.

To my students of karate at both the Toronto Academy of Karate and Judo and the University of Toronto for their patient co-operation during our many photo shoots. I also wish to thank my students at the Calgary Academy of Karate, especially instructor Bruce Winstanley.

To my wife Françoise and my daughters Sonya and Mélina for their help, ideas and encouragement. Thank you most of all for the life we enjoy every day.

Burt Konzak
Toronto, Canada

Table of Contents

*"Hi I'm Mélina!
In self-defense, you learn power over
situations. You don't have to be afraid!"*

*"Hi I'm Sonya!
If you practice well, you can easily learn
these techniques and feel good being
strong, about being yourself!"*

Preface

This outstanding book, written by an internationally recognized expert in the martial arts, presents the basics of self-defense for girls in a step-by-step, easy-to-understand manner.

The book covers many situations that teens encounter in their daily lives, offering preventive measures and avoidance techniques as well as the powerful reactive skills of self-defense. It also includes an appendix for teachers and parents, providing essential background information for understanding the importance of GIRL POWER in a changing world.

As a sociologist specializing in mental health and the family, I find that this book fills an important gap for young women, providing a text that is both practical and intelligent and that is designed for the sophisticated young woman of today.

This book will make a major contribution to the lives of the girls who read it (and their parents such as myself who often worry about their safety). It teaches self-defense and an important philosophy of self-respect that is so important for all of us to possess and to cherish.

Dr. Françoise Boudreau
Director, Department of Sociology
Glendon College
York University, Toronto

"If you think you can, you can.
And if you think you can't,
you're right."

-Mary Kay Ash

THE GIRL POWER IDEAL

Prepare Yourself for the Unexpected

In an ideal world, you would trust everybody, talk to everyone and feel safe wherever you went. Unfortunately, the world we live in isn't quite that simple. Life can truly be unsettling if you find yourself in the wrong place at the wrong time. But there's more to being victimized than fate alone. You can prepare yourself to deal with situations in which you're attacked or confronted by a stranger and learn how to avoid such predicaments altogether. Preparation and know-how are your best defense against any potential attack. Because girls are often victims of assault, this book focuses on settings and contexts that girls often face - the schoolyard, malls, parks, dates, come-ons by total strangers, sexual assault, gang violence and so on. Even if you're a boy... read on! This book is for you too. Anyone can learn and profit from self-defense training.

If you find yourself in a situation in which you feel threatened, it's important to have the knowledge of certain skills and tactics of self-defense that will help you get away safely. Preparation is always your best weapon!

Striking, punching and kicking are skills to be learned and practiced just like heading a ball in soccer or completing a back flip in gymnastics - only the stakes can be much higher. Knowing how, when and where to strike a blow is extremely important and may mean the difference between escaping a confrontation unscathed and suffering a serious injury.

But self-defense is more than simply technique. Physical fitness and activity help a great deal in preparing you to learn how to punch, kick, fall and throw. Relatively simple skills such as learning how to fall are extremely important, but often overlooked in high school and grade school education. However, other sports like volleyball, soccer and gymnastics can be effective in teaching you how to fall and roll properly. In fact, participating in physical activities can help develop many important physical abilities such as speed, strength, agility, flexibility and coordination. The development of these general skills promotes self-confidence and self-assertion in your daily life. Being physically fit thus provides an important foundation for self-defense training.

With specific self-defense training, you develop the mental, physical and spiritual skills necessary to defend yourself. You also develop the personal power required to live your life without feeling weak, helpless or afraid.

The ability to defend yourself is an invaluable tool. Although there won't always be someone there to back you up, taking certain precautions can also go a long way in keeping you safe. Having a plan is smart - do everything possible to avoid being the next victim!

But is violence as common as you think it is? After all, most of you live in a good neighbourhood where violence rarely occurs. Sure there are frightening statistics, but they concern other people, not you! Or do they....

My neighbourhood in Toronto is one of the best - quiet, well lit, safe. Everyone can walk down the street alone at night. But several years ago, a young girl was playing alone in the local park. Her mother had left her there for a matter of minutes - just enough time for a man to run out of his car, grab her and drive away.

Remember, this occurred in the middle of the day, in one of the safest neighbourhoods in the city. We all like to think we live in good communities, but is any neighbourhood or city really safe?

Consider the following true stories. They are very recent and took place in large as well as in small cities. Only the names and places have been changed.

California
Linda White, 18, was jogging along a trail in San Francisco when she was confronted by a man hiding behind a bush. Her body was found the next day.

IT'S A FACT THAT:

● *fifteen is the average age of the first physically violent dating experience;*

● *in Canada, one in every four sex offenders is a teenager;*

● *in an Ontario study, 80% of high school girls reported being harassed in a school setting.*

Texas
Nicole Miller, 13, was a local track and gymnastic sensation in her Dallas hometown. A few summers ago, on a Friday in July, she went to the university stadium to meet a man who had phoned her home proposing to take pictures of her in action for a track magazine. She met with him on the crowded campus - conditions under which her parents felt no reason to be worried. He somehow convinced her to accompany him to a quieter area where they could concentrate on getting the best photos. Two days later, her body was found.

Ontario
In Toronto, police busted a gang of girls at a major high school where they were wreaking havoc on the lives of other girls at the school. There were shakedowns, intimidation, assaults, drugs and other activities you wouldn't associate with getting a quality education.

British Columbia
A gang of girls seeking retribution for supposed offences beat to death a girl in their school.

Florida
Carole, a girl of 14 who studied self-defense through martial arts, was invited to attend a Halloween Party. She told her parents it was at her girlfriend's house and the parents would be home. It was actually at her girlfriend's friend's house and the parents weren't home. There was no trouble... until a group of older boys crashed the party. This is when Carole decided it was time to leave. She ran upstairs to the parents' bedroom to call her father to come and pick her up. Then it happened. Three of the "crashers" stormed into the room and grabbed the phone from her hands. As she resisted, the biggest guy started choking her. Then the thought occurred to her, "I know self-defense." She delivered a punch into her attacker's solar plexus, sending him to the ground. Turning to face the others, she was stunned to see them running from the room. She ran out of the house, went to a neighbour and called her father from there. The neighbour then called the police.

Maryland

Jennie, 15, another student of self-defense, was coming home from school one day by subway with a group of friends. She noticed a man on the train staring at her. When she changed trains and went off by herself, she was distressed to see the man get up and follow her onto the next train. Perhaps it was a coincidence. But when she got off at her stop to walk home, he was right behind her. Now she was anxious and quite nervous, even though it was the middle of the day and the street was full of people. When she passed the supermarket, he suddenly grabbed her from behind and tried to pull her into an adjacent alleyway. Without hesitation, she lifted her leg and kicked him in the groin. She then continued walking home, quite shaken and unsettled, but grateful she knew self-defense.

Notice that in the latter two cases, the girls' knowledge of self-defense enabled them to deal with the situation quickly and effectively. Although mastering a few techniques of self-defense will not make you invincible or invulnerable, when you know self-defense, you're better prepared to help yourself. You truly become more independent and self-reliant.

For each of the scenarios above, consider the following questions:

▶ What were the consequences of the event(s)?

▶ Who was the culprit?

▶ Could the situation have been avoided?

▶ How could she have handled the situation differently?

▶ What would you've done in the same situation?

Discuss the questions with your friends or parents. Then ask yourself these questions after you've worked through this book. You'll see these dangers in a different light and act differently if faced with them yourself. That's what this book is here for! Despite the serious subject matter, you'll find that role-playing and practicing self-defense is fun. And that is the most effective way to learn.

_____

_____

_____

_____

_____

_____

_____

_____

_____

_____

Avoid walking alone in secluded areas.

Attitude and Self-defense

Suppose you're leaving a school party and, as you turn the corner on your way home, three guys are there waiting for you. Of course, they're not waiting for you; they're waiting for their next victim. Before reading further, think about this:

You have the choice to be or not to be a victim. You can say "NO" and, unlike most people, you'll soon have the personal power to back it up! That's what GIRL POWER is about. Anyone can say "NO;" but GIRL POWER gives you the personal power and the means to back it up - with force, if necessary.

Of course, I'm starting with a tough situation - three versus one. How can you possibly win? Well, let's think about another situation: one morning a tiger walks out of her cave to be confronted by a flock of sheep! What does a tiger have to fear from sheep? Simple logic might suggest the sheer force of numbers would give victory to the sheep; they can all jump on the tiger and suffocate her to death.

So, who goes first? Well, the first sheep attacks and becomes lamb chops. Okay, who's second? This is the crucial question. No one wants to be second! The sheep all run for their safety. That is why twenty antelope on the African plains run away from one tiger instead of chasing her. **You're that tiger!** In effect, you're not fighting three attackers; once you strongly take on the first, the others almost invariably retreat. They know a tiger when they see it. In fact, when you become really adept in the skills of self-defense, you can avoid even the first attack. Their instincts will tell them they have chosen the wrong girl. That's what GIRL POWER is all about. With the personal power and know-how of self-defense, you can become a tiger.

What does the scenario described above tell you? Well, it points to the importance of attitude in self-defense - the mental frame of mind that says you won't be defeated and you'll never give up! The next challenge is to transfer this attitude into action: how you walk, how you look at someone and how you react in fearful situations. In other words, your body language and expressions must all show you can achieve whatever you want in life. By building confidence with know-how, you can never be defeated.

Keep your
eyes open

Learn to walk tall. It projects confidence.

PERSONAL ASSESSMENT:
My Preventive Self-defense Checklist

Read each statement below. Circle the number of the response that best reflects your current behaviour. This checklist will help you assess your preventive self-defense behaviours and provide you with a general impression of how these behaviours can be changed or maintained to enhance your personal safety. Add the points received and refer to the descriptions at the end of the quiz to interpret your scores.

	Almost Always	Sometimes	Never
▶ I avoid being with people I don't really trust.	2	1	0
▶ I avoid being with people who try pushing me into doing things I don't want to do like taking drugs, drinking, smoking or having sex.	2	1	0
▶ When travelling at night, especially late at night, I try to go with a friend or have a parent pick me up.	2	1	0
▶ I avoid situations I consider dangerous such as entering an elevator alone with a strange man or accepting a ride from a stranger.	2	1	0
▶ I avoid going alone to the apartment of someone I don't know well.	2	1	0
▶ When conversing with a stranger on the Internet or via e-mail, I'm careful to never give out my name or other personal information.	2	1	0
▶ I'm careful not to take things at face value.	2	1	0
▶ I'm careful not to accept drinks that have already been opened.	2	1	0
▶ I'm aware of my surroundings.	2	1	0
▶ I tell someone (a parent or close friend) where I'm going.	2	1	0

Preventive self-defense score: _____

Interpreting Your Scores

16-20 : Excellent! You're aware of the importance of preventive self-defense. If you continue these habits, this area shouldn't pose a serious risk.

11-15 : Your preventive self-defense practices in this area are good, but there's room for improvement. Even a small change may help you enhance your safety.

6-10 : Some safety risks are showing. You may need more information about the risks and why it's important for you to change these behaviours.

0-5 : You may be taking serious and unnecessary risks. If you're not aware of the risks or what to do about them, you can easily get the information and help you need to improve.

Requirements for Effective Self-defense

In practicing self-defense, many variables must be considered for achieving optimal results, including attaining and maintaining a high level of physical and mental health. Making healthy choices such as participating in regular physical activity, avoiding alcohol and other drugs and following good nutritional advice are important guidelines to consider (see My Health and Lifestyle Assessment Survey on pages 26–29).

Exercise
Participating in regular exercise effectively improves strength, flexibility, endurance, agility and coordination. The development of these general skills also promotes self-confidence, providing an important foundation for self-defense training.

Engaging in physical exercise and self-defense will initiate a cycle that will help you control your weight, protect yourself against various diseases, boost your energy level, manage stress and anxiety and improve your self-esteem. It may also be the diversion you need to avoid trouble and develop the discipline and mental toughness required to keep yourself safe. As you continue to participate in these activities, you'll gradually experience increased fitness, positive shifts in your nutritional habits, increased vigor and a strong sense of self-empowerment - all of which breed self-confidence (see Figure opposite page).

So take the opportunity to enhance your physical conditioning by taking a self-defense or fitness course at your school, local Y or other fitness organization. If you have any type of health problem or concern, consult your physician before beginning a self-defense or physical fitness program

Self-confidence cycle.

...the more I do...

- confident
- empowered
- positive

- exercise
- activity
- play

- negative
- reckless
- low esteem

- fatigue
- tense
- fat

...the better I am...

...the better I get...

- relaxed
- vigorous
- happy

- physical activity
- energy
- strength

- depressed
- anxious
- crabby

- sick
- tired
- hungry

...the better I feel...

Nutrition

Nutrition is another important variable to consider in developing your full potential. Some diets are associated with disease states or illness, while others are linked with energy and vigor. While all foods are good to eat, some are good to eat more often than others. Following the basic rules of variety, balance and moderation will effectively guide you to eating sensibly.

Any way you put it, nutrition has profound effects on your general health and well-being, which also affects your ability to learn and execute the skills of self-defense most effectively and with confidence.

Practice

The capabilities of the human body seem endless. You have witnessed the powerful, yet graceful movements that define world-class athletes in various sports. However, don't forget the important role of regular and continued practice in the mastery of these techniques. The same holds true for techniques of self-defense.

Almost all the techniques you'll learn are surprisingly easy and effective. But remember: practice makes perfect. In a crisis, you have little time to think and must be able to act instinctively. And acting instinctively means having confidence in yourself and your abilities. With this attitude, anything is possible.

Self-control

After learning the formidable skills used in self-defense, remember the importance of self-control when working with a partner. Make sure you both understand what the other is doing - who is attacking and who is defending. Practice the techniques in the book diligently, but always with self-control. And always make safety your first priority - never do anything you believe is too difficult for you.

Make sure that when you're working
with a partner you stop 3-5 centimeters
(1-2 inches) from your target area to
prevent injury.

PERSONAL ASSESSMENT:
Evaluating My Health and Lifestyle

What does it mean to be healthy? We all have the desire to achieve health and wellness, but many of us don't know how to achieve it. This brief personal profile will help you assess your health behaviours and provide you with a general impression of how these behaviours can be changed or maintained to enhance your personal health status. For each statement below, circle the number of the response that best reflects your behaviour. Add the points received for each section and refer to the descriptions at the end of the quiz to interpret your scores.

Exercise/Fitness

	Almost Always	Sometimes	Never
▶ I engage in moderate exercise for 20 to 60 minutes, 3 to 5 times a week.	3	1	0
▶ I maintain a healthy weight, avoiding overweight and underweight.	3	1	0
▶ I do exercises to develop muscular strength and endurance at least twice a week.	2	1	0
▶ I spend some of my leisure time participating in physical activities.	2	1	0

Exercise/Fitness Score: _____

Nutrition

	Almost Always	Sometimes	Never
▶ I eat a variety of foods each day in an attempt to eat a balanced diet, including 5 or more servings of fruits and vegetables.	3	1	0
▶ I limit the amount of fat, particularly saturated fat, in my diet.	3	1	0
▶ I avoid skipping meals.	2	1	0
▶ I try to balance my caloric intake with my activity level.	2	1	0

Nutrition Score: _____

	Almost Always	Sometimes	Never

Safety

	Almost Always	Sometimes	Never
▶ I wear a seat belt while riding in a car.	3	I	0
▶ I avoid driving while under the influence of alcohol or other drugs and I avoid riding with persons who are.	3	I	0
▶ I select appropriate equipment for all activities and maintain equipment in good working order.	2	I	0
▶ I learn procedures and precautions before undertaking new recreational or other activities.	2	I	0

Safety Score: _____

Sleep, Rest and Relaxation

	Almost Always	Sometimes	Never
▶ I plan my schedule to allow time for leisure activities.	2	I	0
▶ I plan my daily schedule to allow time for contemplation, meditation or prayer.	2	I	0
▶ I get between 7 and 8 hours of sleep daily.	2	I	0
▶ I avoid using sleep-inducing over-the-counter drugs.	2	I	0
▶ I curtail activities when I need to recover from illness or injury.	2	I	0

Sleep, Rest and Relaxation Score: _____

	Almost Always	Sometimes	Never
Tobacco Use			

If you never use tobacco, enter a score of 10 for this section and go to the next section.

	Almost Always	Sometimes	Never
▶ I avoid using tobacco.	2	1	0
▶ I smoke only low-tar-and-nicotine cigarettes, a pipe or cigars or I use smokeless tobacco.	2	1	0

Tobacco Use Score: _____

Alcohol and Other Drugs

	Almost Always	Sometimes	Never
▶ I avoid alcohol or I drink infrequently and in limited amounts.	4	1	0
▶ I avoid using alcohol or other drugs as a way of handling stressful situations or problems in my life.	2	1	0
▶ I limit contact with others who are using alcohol or other drugs.	2	1	0
▶ I take prescription drugs only in the manner prescribed and use over-the-counter drugs only in accordance with directions.	2	1	0

Alcohol and Other Drugs Score: _____

Emotional Health	Almost Always	Sometimes	Never
▶ I enjoy being a student and have a job or do other work I like.	2	1	0
▶ I find it easy to relax and express my feelings freely.	2	1	0
▶ I manage stress well.	2	1	0
▶ I have close friends, relatives or others I can talk to about personal matters or ask for help.	2	1	0
▶ I participate in group activities or hobbies I enjoy.	2	1	0

Emotional Health Score: _____

Interpreting Your Scores

9-10 : Excellent! You're aware of the importance of this area of wellness and practice good health habits. As long as you continue these habits, this area shouldn't pose a serious health risk.

6-8 : Your health practices in this area are good, but there's room for improvement. Even a small change may help you achieve high-level health.

3-5 : Some health risks are showing. You may need more information about the risks and why it's important for you to change these behaviours.

0-2 : You may be taking serious and unnecessary risks with your health. If you're not aware of the risks or what to do about them, you can easily get the information and help you need to improve.

"In violence, we forget who we are."

-Mary McCarthy

DO I NEED A WEAPON?

Under the law, you're not allowed to carry weapons such as pistols or revolvers. There is also a great risk of accidental injury. You'd also be in big trouble if an attacker took the gun from you!

Nunchakus and knuckle-dusters are also forbidden. So are pepper sprays. It's also against the law to bring knives, stars and truncheons along with you to school. An attacker can use these weapons against you if he happens to get his hands on them.

Think about the following:

- *How does the girl in the picture feel?*
- *Do the guys believe she would shoot them?*
- *Would you really shoot if you had to?*
- *What use is a gun if it only shoots blanks?*
- *What would happen to the girl if she lost the gun?*
- *What happens if the guy takes the gun away from the girl?*
- *Would you carry a gun around with you all day?*
- *Would you take a gun to school with you?*
- *What could an attacker use against you if he took it from you or you lost it?*

"If I have a weapon, no one can do anything to me!"

Fashion power!
Use your heels

Besides, you have other weapons in your bag. A book, a key, a comb, or a corkscrew may seem harmless, but they can be potentially useful if a situation should arise.

Don't hit someone over the head with an umbrella, book or poster; it's useless! Instead, poke him in the face or neck with the corner of your textbook. This is a good technique using a rather "innocent" weapon.

A key dragged across the face is very painful. Moreover, the resulting scar makes it easier for the police to find your attacker. Another option you have is to thrust a key into his eye. But ask yourself: are there perhaps better ways for most situations?

If he grabs you, stab his hand with your key or a pen or slice the teeth of your comb across his eyes.

How effective is the can of hair spray you carry in your purse?

A can of hair spray might work, but it gives one a false sense of security. There's much to be said against it:

▶ Older spray cans often lose their pressure.

▶ It's not always effective (e.g., against someone wearing glasses).

▶ If the wind is against you, the gas will spray into your own face.

▶ Operating the can under the stress of a dangerous situation isn't so easy.

▶ Many women and girls end up getting sprayed with their own cans.

What if the man who grabs you from behind turns out to be your uncle, but you only realize it after you have sliced his eyes with the teeth of your comb? Will the police be impressed with your resourcefulness, or appalled at your excessive reaction?

Learning self-defense may not be an easy or obvious task, but it's not as difficult as you may believe. The following chapters will focus on techniques that really work and are realistic - techniques that are easily learned and effective.

Think about the following:

● *When would you resort to these measures?*

● *Would they be okay to use during an incident at school?*

"The great crises of life aren't,
I think, necessarily those which are in themselves
the hardest to bear,
but those for which we are least prepared."

-Mary Adams

LEARNING TO STRIKE, PUNCH AND KICK

The Foundation of Self-defense

Because your attacker is likely to be bigger and stronger than you are, you might think he has the initial advantage. Never underestimate your own strength or the strength of the human spirit. Not only do you have the power of right on your side, you also have the element of surprise! He might be bigger and stronger, but the last thing he expects is your strong spirited response. The element of surprise coupled with the speed of your response is a formidable combination. Add this to a solid foundation in self-defense and you can't be beaten.

There are three important points to remember for any self-defense: 1. balance and self-control; 2. spirit in the eyes; and 3. the specific technique (e.g., a punch).

Balance
Balance and self-control are the basis for all self-defense techniques. Much of what you'll do is oriented towards "unbalancing" your attacker. In other words, you want to catch him by surprise. Balance and good posture will help to maximize the effectiveness of your technique.

Spirit in the Eyes
Strong spirit in the eyes communicates to your attacker that you aren't intimidated and you won't back down. This is the first step to "unbalancing" your attacker.

Technique: Your Tool for Self-defense
In many situations, you can avert danger by breaking free and getting away or simply running from the start. However, if you must fight, your technique must be effective. For that to happen, you must practice. You must also pay close attention to aiming your punches and kicks so each one is effective. It's important to understand that if a punch or kick doesn't hurt, it's pointless.

Learning the proper punching technique is important.

The Punch

The punch is the basic self-defense skill used in many dangerous situations. A proper punch requires a tight fist. This helps you avoid injuring your fingers.

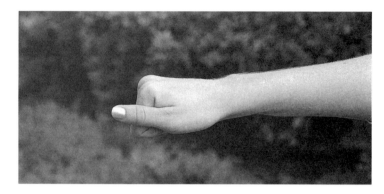

The thumb shouldn't be held inside the fist or stick out where it can be broken.

If the fist is held loose, you'll hurt your fingers. Make sure it's tight.

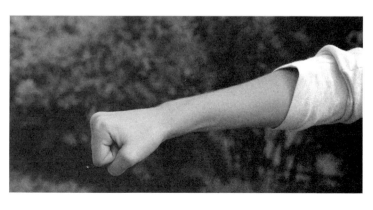

The wrist must be held straight, the fingers tight and the thumb held underneath the fist.

"Oh yeah...

don't forget to pull in your thumb!"

The steps to making a proper fist.

To execute an effective punch follow these four steps:

Step 1
Punch from the hip on a straight line directly into the solar plexus, a vulnerable pressure point in the body. Begin with the fist in a palm-up position; then twist the forearm so the palm faces down to complete the punch. This screwdriver-like action adds power to the punch. Make sure you keep the elbow close to the body while punching. To avoid an injury (tennis elbow) do not completely extend your elbow as you punch.

Step 2
Concentrate on punching with the first two knuckles; like the head of a hammer, it focuses your power. Scream or yell as you punch. The loud noise will have an unsettling effect on your attacker, so use it to your advantage. As you yell, tighten your stomach muscles and exhale sharply. Use the power of your abdomen.

Step 3
As you punch, pull the other hand back to the hip. This enables you to use the power of both arms instead of one, much like a baseball pitcher who simultaneously pulls his left arm back as he throws with his right arm. In addition, your other arm is in position ready to punch again if necessary. This element of speed is essential - be prepared to strike several times, without hesitation.

Step 4
When it comes to punching, speed is more important than mass - size doesn't always matter. First, practice slowly and patiently to perfect the form of your technique. Then, gradually increase your speed.

    This may seem like a lot to remember, but that's why you have to practice! Only practice will make self-defense instinctive. When you practice punching, try to visualize situations where you might use it.
    Practice punching into a punching mitt, an old baseball glove, a medicine ball or even a mat against the wall. Start slowly and make sure you're holding your wrist straight. If you're ever approached from the front, aim for the solar plexus, tip of the nose or groin; if facing someone from the side, you can strike the ribs or head.

Learn to prepare...

...then strike!

Practice into a punching mitt.

Practice into a medicine ball.

The Palm Heel Strike

If an attacker grabs you anywhere below the throat or if he's much taller than you, you may not have a clear shot at his solar plexus. In this situation, you can use an effective palm heel strike (or a punch) to the face. Just like executing a punch, strike from your hip on a straight line directly to his face - only this time, your weapon is the heel of your hand. As in the punch to the solar plexus, the precise place you strike is important. Focus your blow either to the chin or the tip of the nose.

What can I do when I'm grabbed by the neck?

I can use a palm heel strike to the chin.

Practice the palm heel strike against a mat on the wall or any other appropriate target such as a baseball glove, medicine ball, etc.

When hitting with the palm heel of your right hand, take a step forward with your left foot.

Extend your left arm towards your target and pull your right arm back next to your body. Bend your hand right up. Then, using the force of your entire body hit the target hard with the palm heel of the right hand.

Hitting with the Knife Edge of the Hand

If you need to hit from a different angle, an effective strike is the "knife hand attack." The striking area is the side of the hand below the little finger. Hit the side of the neck - a very effective pressure point.

Strike down with the little finger side of the hand as you would with a knife.

Keep your fingers together and your thumb in (protected). Move your entire body into the attack and pull your other hand back, poised to strike the attacker directly into the solar plexus if necessary.

Practice hitting the medicine ball as you rotate your body into the attack.

"The knife hand attack isn't only powerful and effective, it's also easy to learn!"

The knife hand is a very powerful and effective technique. You can easily break a board as demonstrated in this photo.

The Knee Kick

Suppose your attacker grabs your arms, what would you do? If you can't punch, use another part of your body - like your legs. The knee kick is so simple that an explanation of how to do it is virtually unnecessary. Just remember: put power into the kick and aim directly for the groin - a well-focused kick always works!

Knee kick a medicine ball for practice. It's also a lot of fun working with a partner.

"... knee kick him!"

Notice how even a small girl choked in the schoolyard by one of the big boys can defend herself with a knee kick. He'll think twice before attacking her again!

Put your running shoes to good use... get out of the situation as fast as possible!

Yes, it hurts; and yes, it will stop him. Boys are often hit in the groin accidentally and they know the feeling - something guys don't want to experience again. So, when you need to, use it!

The Kick

It's important to master the kicking technique because it's useful against bigger opponents. The long reach of the legs becomes a great equalizer. Initially, it may be awkward to kick because you might feel like you're losing your balance. Be patient. Practice will bring rapid progress. Just remember to keep your base foot flat on the ground and your knee bent. This gives you greater stability during the execution of the kick. The kick has three basic steps as illustrated below.

Step 1
Raise the knee ready to kick, bending the toes up for maximum power keeping the foot as close to the thigh as possible.

Step 2
Thrust your foot forward from the knee as you yell, keeping the toes up.

Step 3
Pull the kick back and quickly return the foot to the ground to maintain your balance.

It's important to pull your toes up so you hit the target with the ball of your foot, otherwise you risk injuring your toes. By bending the toes, your calf muscle also tenses, giving you greater power.

Practice kicking a medicine ball. Hitting the target accurately is important. Aim for the knee or shin to avoid losing your balance and to prevent your attacker from grabbing your leg! A lower kick is also hard to block. All the kicks become easier and stronger with practice.

Front kick into a medicine ball.

The Elbow Strike

A forward elbow strike to the solar plexus, ribs or kidneys or a higher strike to the head is a very powerful technique for fighting in close contact. Thrust your entire body forward and pull your right hand back for greater power and in preparation for the next strike.

Practice the elbow strike into a medicine ball.

A rear elbow strike would also be an effective defense against a rear choke attack.

Now you know how to strike, punch and kick to defend yourself. Of course, it's always better if you can get out of a dangerous situation without having to use these techniques. But if you must defend yourself, use all your power and will to hit your attacker with everything you have. Don't hold back!

You're now well prepared should an attacker present himself; but in order to get the most out of self-defense training, you must practice. It takes effort, but the rewards are enormous!

"You must do the thing
you think you can't do."

-Eleanor Roosevelt

LEARNING TO TAKE A DIVE

Although you may have occasion to apply some of the techniques in this book in actual self-defense situations, the one you'll probably use the most is the falling technique. Whether playing sports at school, riding your bike, kidding with friends or actually fighting with someone, the risk of falling is always present. This is one way you may get seriously injured. A back or neck injury, a concussion or a broken arm are typical injuries resulting from falls. Therefore, it's crucial to learn the proper way to fall in self-defense!

Taking a dive! It's a good thing you know how to fall.

Ironically, very few situations requiring knowledge of falling stem from physical confrontations with others; falls tend to occur during activities such as skiing, ice-skating, bicycling and mountain climbing. You'll be surprised at how courageous you feel once you learn how to fall properly. Start by practicing on a mat and progress slowly. Courage is different than recklessness!

You may have already learned how to roll in phys. ed. period classes. Unfortunately, many schools no longer teach these fundamental skills. Remember:

▶ Your first priority is to protect your head, whether you're practicing rolling or falling. To do so, tuck your chin in tightly as if you were making yourself into a little ball and keep your eyes on your belly button.

▶ Your arms (not your head) should bear the major impact of your fall the moment you hit the ground.

▶ Always exhale when you land. This will greatly diminish the impact of the fall!

Side Fall

When you fall, use your arm to absorb most of the impact, landing with the palm down, the arm straight and at an angle of approximately 45 degrees from the body. Notice that the eyes are on the belly button, which can only be seen when the head is up and thus protected. Never let your head hit the ground. On a mat, it may not hurt too much; but on the street, it can be devastating!

From a sitting position on a mat or on soft ground like a thick lawn bring your right arm (palm down) to your left shoulder.

Practice the side fall on both the right and left sides.

Back Fall

Back fall uses many of the same principles as the side fall. Follow the steps as shown in the photos.

From a sitting position on a mat, bring both your arms up across the chest, palms facing down.

"Breath out when you fall!"

As you fall keep your chin tucked in.

When you land, slap both hands hard on
the mat, absorbing most of the impact of
the fall. Keep your palms down, elbows straight
and your arms at a 45-degree angle from your
body. Your eyes should be on
your belly button and your chin tucked in
to protect your head.

Front Fall

The front fall is an uncomfortable technique to practice, but it's important. And it can't be avoided when someone pulls your feet out from under you or you fall forward while skiing or ice-skating. Without this exercise, you'll either hit your head, smash your knees or break your arms as you fall.

"Ouch, don't land on your knees!"

Practice in a kneeling position with your hands (palms forward) in front of your face. As you land, protect your head by turning your face to the side.

Remember, protecting your head is always your first priority. Don't land on your knees, but on your arms and the balls of your feet. No other part of the body is touching the ground. Your arms should absorb the major impact of the fall.

"Keep your focus!"

Put your hands up in preparation for the fall if you're pushed down. You can also subtly move your right leg to kick an attacker in the groin even as you're being pushed down.

Forward Roll

The forward roll helps in many instances when you fall forward from a bicycle or while skiing. It can prevent many serious injuries by taking the impact off your head or another vulnerable part of the body.

Begin by taking a step forward with your right foot, bending down and placing your left hand parallel to your right foot. Place your right hand between your right foot and left hand. Tuck your chin in to protect your head.

Begin your roll, keeping along the right shoulder with your chin tucked in.

Finish your roll, bringing your left arm down onto the mat in the same position as the side fall. During the entire roll, your eyes stay on your belly button.

"This above all, to refuse to be a victim."

-Margaret Atwood

AT SCHOOL AND AT THE MALL

Think about this

- *How often do boys fight?*
- *Why do they fight?*
- *How often do you see girls fighting?*
- *Why do girls fight? How do they fight?*
- *Do boys and girls fight each other?*
- *What are the main reasons for such fights?*
- *How do they end?*
- *Has this happened to you?*
- *What did you feel like when it happened?*
- *What do you think the boys feel like in such circumstances?*

You don't need a television to see a schoolyard brawl. You can probably see one any day of the week at your school.

Have you ever seen someone beaten up by a boy or girl or by more than one person? Are there "gangs" at your school or in your area? What is the point of these gangs?

Are there some fights that are okay? Which ones are wrong? Are fights at your school dangerous? Do you try to get out of such situations without resorting to violence?

Think about this

- *Why do some kids not recognize any limits when they're fighting to the point that someone ends up getting hurt?*

- *How can you protect yourself against gangs that steal expensive jackets, shoes and pocket money?*

- *How do you avoid getting involved in gang wars in your neighbourhood or school?*

- *What do you do when you get caught in the middle of a fight between gangs?*

Make a call if you're in trouble or you need assistance. No money is required to call *911* or *0* (operator).

Look at the boys in this photo. They're looking for a suitable victim. Have you ever seen this look?

How Do Fights in the Schoolyard Differ From One Another?

▶ Guys sometimes confront one another or pick on one individual.

▶ Boys have arguments that sometimes quickly escalate into violence.

▶ The hierarchy within a clique or a class can be established through fighting - this tends to be more of a problem with boys.

▶ Boys and girls often seek contact, but are afraid to go up to one another just to talk.

Sometimes boys can think of more "dramatic" ways to impress and talk with girls. They may put their arms around you, tease you, grab you or generally harass you. They may even think you like it.

This kind of thing has always occurred. Schoolyard supervision, good intentions and punishments from parents and the school can never completely eliminate these conflicts.

You're harassed by a gang of girls at school. You show fear and begin to cry. Not knowing what to do and being clearly outnumbered and overpowered, you'll easily give in to their demands.

Think about this

● *Why did the gang choose to pick on this girl in particular?*

A gang of girls is threatening you.

Role-playing

Two to three girls pretend to be gang members who threaten you. You don't like it. Make this clear to them! How do you do that? How would you stand while talking to them - slouching and/or hunched over or tall and straight? How would your eyes look - like you're about to cry or full of power and fury? What do you do if that doesn't work? Is running away a good option? Why or why not? What would happen if other girls took your side? Is this a possibility? If not, why couldn't it happen? Why can't girls help each other, even in a threatening situation?

Some situations aren't as threatening; however, more and more violent scenarios arise amongst teens that are dangerous and even life threatening. A few years ago, girl gangs were an oddity. Now, they're increasingly common - and dangerous.

Bear in Mind

❿ Stay alert to such dangers and avoid these situations.

❿ There's no shame in moving away from such dangers when they threaten you!

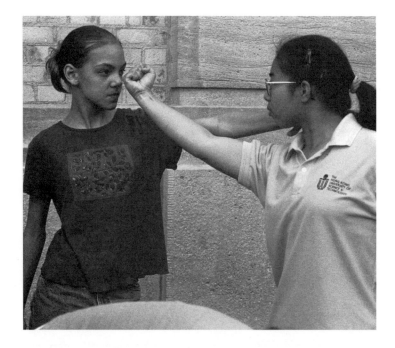

If you do end up in a dangerous situation, sometimes there's only one way to get out of it: hit your attacker with all your might and get away quickly. Then call the police.

▶ Get help when classmates are threatened or hurt.

▶ Assaults, theft and blackmail are criminal offenses. If you report them or make a statement to the police, you're not being a snitch.

Getting out of Someone's Grasp

Sometimes when you ignore a boy's attempts to get your attention, he'll grab you by the wrist or arm. Often, all you need to do is free yourself firmly and the boy will get the message.

Even strong boys have weak spots that you can exploit. If you're held by the wrist, their weakest point is between the thumb and forefinger. You can free yourself from their grasp by focusing on this spot and twisting towards the thumb. We call this "killing the thumb." Don't use just your arm strength; twist your entire body to pull your arm loose in the direction of the thumb.

Practice using this way of freeing yourself against different holds on your wrist. Switch partners often so you learn to break free of different kinds of holds, including strong ones.

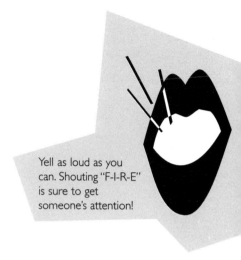

Yell as loud as you can. Shouting "F-I-R-E" is sure to get someone's attention!

An attacker grabs both your wrists, which is particularly difficult to handle.

Always move your wrists in the direction of his thumb...

...and then break loose.

You can also use the knee kick to the groin to free yourself and escape.

"... run!!!"

Break free of a hold on your arm by twisting your body away powerfully.

"Oh... he's not going to like that!"

If he continues to pursue you, hit him with the back of your first two knuckles.

If he continues to pursue you, you can also follow through with a back-fist to the nose. First, bring your hand to the opposite shoulder, then strike his face, moving your arm across your body to build up momentum for the blow. Hit him with the back of your first two knuckles. Remember that speed is more important than mass. A tiny bullet fired from a gun is deadly, but thrown would most likely prove harmless. The velocity of your punch will count more than your attacker's size.

A boy grabs your hair.

Pull your left arm to your hip and...

...punch him in the solar plexus.

It works!

Read the scenarios below. After reading each scenario, think about what you would do or how you would react in the same situation. Could it have been avoided? What else could you have done?

The Headlock

You're being held in a headlock. Instead of waving your right arm around aimlessly or pushing his head in futility, push your thumb right into his throat. That will get you quick results. You can follow through with a right punch to the ribs or kidneys; both areas are open for attack. Or use the punch alone without using the thumb-in-the-throat technique. As you learn more self-defense techniques, you'll have more options at your disposal. But don't get hung up on the choices! React quickly and confidently.

Push your thumb into your attacker's throat.

At The Water Fountain

As you go for a drink of water, an attacker is hiding in the bushes behind you. While your back is turned, he grabs you. He'll be surprised when you kick him on the instep, drive your elbow into his ribs and thrust your fist into his groin. Remember: you don't need all these techniques - any one will do. But learn more options so you can judge the situation and decide what you want to do. Plus, if he blocks your first attempt, you're always ready to follow through with more techniques.

If attacked from behind while at the water fountain you can...

kick him on the instep or...

elbow him in the ribs or...

punch him in the groin.

Books aren't just for reading...

they make an effective weapon!

On Your Way Home

On the way home from school, book in hand, you're accosted by an older classmate. He tries to grab you by the waist, pulling you in closer. Don't let go of the book; it makes a simple but effective weapon.

Shove your textbook into his nose.

On the Playground

Some "weapons" are easy to find and available around you with a little insight. Suppose you're playing with your little sister on the slide when an older man tries to embrace you. Quickly reach down to the sand and throw some of it in his face. Then run. You could also kick him in the groin with your foot (which is in front of his groin and ready to strike).

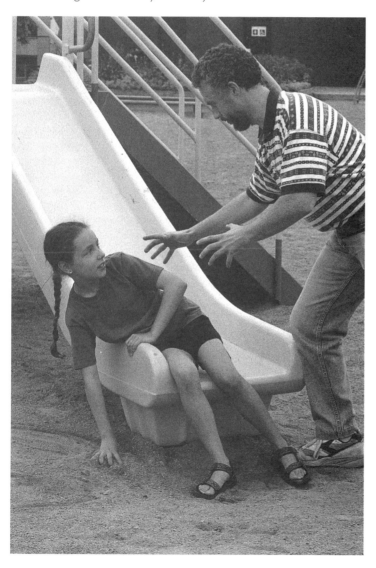

Throw sand into his eyes.

In the Schoolyard

In the schoolyard an older guy grabs your shoulder. Thrust your thumb into his throat to push him away. He'll quickly let go and move back.

Someone grabs you by the shoulder.

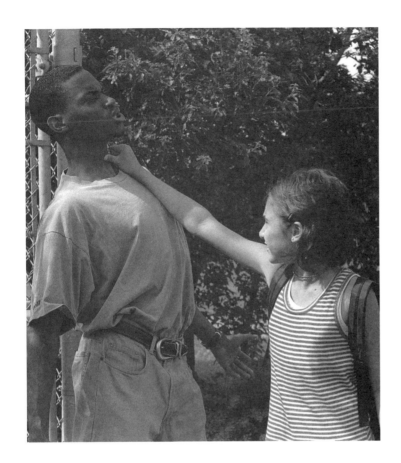

You can thrust your thumb
into his throat.

Tell a teacher

Boys Who Kick

A boy tries to kick you as you pass by. You spontaneously block with a kick into his ankle. This "kicking block" will hurt and he'll have no stomach for further aggression against you.

Block a kick with a kick.

You shouldn't hesitate to come to the aid of other girls in trouble. It takes courage, but you'll have a friend for life. The ideal first thing to do is to call or run for help. At school, a loud scream will always bring immediate attention - and attention from others will often drive the attacker away. Get the principal, a teacher, a security guard or anyone who can help. At the mall, ask someone to help, find the security guard or call 911. Take charge of the situation! It doesn't always mean fighting.

Taking off the Hair

While walking with a friend, she's suddenly attacked. You might be shocked, but don't stand by idly. Grab the attacker's hair and pull him down. As his hair goes down, so goes his head; and the rest immediately follows. We call this "taking off the hair" or "scalping." You don't pull his hair; you take it off - and down he goes!

A friend's being attacked. What do you do?

Grab the attacker's hair and pull him down.

81

Taking off the Ear

Suppose your attacker has no hair. No problem - simply "take off the ear." He'll quickly follow. On his way down, your friend can join in with a knee kick to the groin.

You can also grab the attacker's ear.

"Oh... He's not going to like this either!"

Your friend is joining in with a knee kick to the groin.

Three is Better Than One

It's reassuring to be able to help one another out and to have friends you can count on. It's also nice to be a friend that your friends can count on in return. That's one of the great advantages of knowing self-defense.

Tell a friend!

The attacker is about to strike your friend. You and another friend immediately come to her aid and...

grab one leg each.

Down he goes!

"When you're frightened don't sit still,
keep on doing something.
The act of doing will give you back
your courage."

-Grace Ogot

PROTECTING YOUR BOUNDARIES

The "Come-on"

You know the scenario: someone comes on to you and won't leave you alone. He sweet talks you, asks you out repeatedly, follows you home, writes lewd letters and does other things that bother you. Then again, sometimes you like it when a nice guy comes up to talk to you. But there's a difference! The purpose of this chapter is to develop strategies to defuse potentially dangerous situations before they escalate.

The preparation involved in these exercises isn't physical, but mental. Because no one response is correct for all situations, you need to think out alternative plans of action before encountering these potentially dangerous circumstances. By engaging in these "thought exercises," you greatly reduce the risk of having to resort to physical techniques of self-defense. The best route is still prevention and avoidance.

The "come-on."

My Personal Space Checklist

In order to explore what you find comfortable and uncomfortable, complete the boundaries worksheet below. Next to each item, indicate a check in the appropriate column that applies to you.

	Nice	Okay	Don't Know	Stupid	Disgusting
giving presents					
whistling					
pinching your bum					
necking					
cuddling					
holding tight					
groping					
sleeping with each other					
snuggling					
pet names/ endearments					
grabbing					
looks					
kissing					
hugging					
stroking					
staring					
threatening					
hitting					
flirting					
trying to have sex after you say "NO"					

Are some responses better than others? Does your decision depend on where, what or whom you have in mind when you think about each term? Maybe it's more appropriate to make a different set of responses for different types of guys.

Take a closer look at the terms to which you responded "don't know." I don't know is always a troublesome answer. It always risks being taken the wrong way; if you're not sure about something or you feel pressured, say "NO" clearly and firmly. Other responses such as: "I DON'T WANT TO DO THIS," "STOP IT," "STOP NOW," "LET GO," "IT'S TIME TO LEAVE..." can also get your point across. But say it like you mean it! You must always be firm in the decisions you make. And when necessary, leave! Get out of the situation before things get out of hand.

The Distance Game

Play out the following situation: Someone's approaching you and you don't want him to come any closer. Using strong eye contact and confident body language, make yourself clear: this is the limit. Don't come any closer!

If you succeed in showing people how close they can come to you, you'll avoid a number of uncomfortable situations!

What else could you do?

If you have a
cell phone,
use it.

Riding Public Transit

Play out the following situation:
You're riding on the bus or subway. Without asking, a boy sits down beside you and starts coming on to you. You want to be left alone.

What else could you do?

You could:

● *go sit somewhere else;*

● *tell him clearly you're not interested;*

● *ask the bus or subway driver for help;*

● *start to complain loudly;*

● *call out something to embarrass him like: "This guy obviously needs a girlfriend. Any volunteers?"*

In the Café

Play out the same scenario above as if you were in a café.

You could:

● *find another place to sit;*

● *tell him clearly you're not interested and would like to be left alone;*

● *refuse to acknowledge any of his looks and act as if he isn't there;*

● *ask a café patron for assistance;*

● *complain loudly so other people hear;*

● *tell him you're expecting a friend to join you shortly.*

What else could you do?

_____

_____

_____

_____

_____

_____

_____

_____

Carry enough money
for public transit
and a phone call.

At the Swimming Pool or Beach

Play out the following scenario:
You and a group of girlfriends found a nice spot at the beach when a couple of guys come and settle down beside you. They make stupid remarks, tell you what cute "babes" you are and try to impress you with all kinds of gross comments.

What else could you do?

YOU COULD:

- take your towel and move somewhere else;

- tell them clearly and calmly you'd like to be left alone;

- claim your boyfriend or some guys from your class are coming to meet you soon;

- make fun of them loud enough for everyone to hear;

- send one of you off to get help from lifeguards or other officials;

- give them the cold shoulder, refuse to acknowledge any of their looks and act as if they aren't there.

Being Followed

Imagine it's evening and you're returning home from practice. On the way, you notice that someone is following you. You're alone on the street. What do you do?

Hail a cab if necessary. You can pay when you get home safely if you don't have enough money with you

What else could you do?

YOU COULD:

● *cross the street and see what happens. Does he follow you;*

● *stop and stand in an area where you see there are a lot of people;*

● *go into a store;*

● *call home or the police;*

● *carry a whistle or yell for help.*

WHAT HAPPENS IF:

- *You take the letter to the guidance counsellor or principal right away?*

- *After class, you calmly tell the person who sent it to please leave you alone?*

- *You threaten to go to the principal or guidance counsellor with the letter if this continues?*

- *You show the letter to your friends and say something negative about the person who sent it like, "Why does this guy find it necessary to send me such a disgusting letter?"*

Receiving A Letter

Imagine you're at school and during class you receive a letter that's slanderous or too personal. Develop ideas about what you could do in this situation.

What else could you do?

_____

_____

_____

_____

_____

_____

_____

_____

Be Prepared

You should be able to come up with other good ways to handle these scenarios. Are some behaviours "better" than others? Why? Let your imagination run free.

It's good to think about such scenarios and your potential responses to them in advance rather than on the spot. That way you won't have to grope for responses when the situation arises. From the guy's point of view, seeing this uncertainty encourages him further and gives him the confidence to continue harassing you. Thus, your ability to respond calmly and intelligently, with dignity and firmness, will go a long way in keeping guys like this at bay. If a boy is interesting and you're impressed, let him know. But if you're not interested, you must also let him know - leave no doubt in his mind you want nothing to do with him!

Once again, it's wise to plan out in advance what you would or could do in a similar situation. Don't leave it for the heat of the moment when you may not be thinking your clearest and may be anxious. Prevention is always your best option: walk home with friends, have someone pick you up or choose a busy, well-lit route.

But even the best preventive measures can't eliminate risk. Always be prepared for the unexpected. And remember self-defense techniques should always be your last option, when all others have been exhausted. It's not pleasant to hit someone, but if you must, hit him with everything you have. Never hold back!

It's a good idea to talk to friends and parents to get their ideas as well. It helps to listen to the experiences of others in developing your own plan of action. Planning allows you to be clear and assertive in your responses. Make no mistake - your attacker will get the message: NO means NO!

"Nobody is as powerful
as we make them out to be."

-Alice Walker

SEXUAL HARASSMENT AND DATING

The Dirty Old Man

Most people are repelled when they conjure up images of a dirty old man. However, there are dirty young men as well. These men may be handsome, charming and well dressed, but don't let this front deceive you. It's wise to always be alert!

Therefore, think twice before you:

● *walk or go anywhere with strangers;*

● *get into conversations with strangers;*

● *let strangers give you any gifts;*

● *accept a drink from a stranger;*

● *get into a car with a stranger;*

● *go to the apartment of a guy you don't know well.*

Dirty old man hidden in the bushes.

These are simple preventive measures based on common sense; yet, the issue isn't as simple as it may seem. Recognizing sexual harassment right away is often impossible.

Why do we even have to talk about this issue? Isn't the stranger easy to spot?

The image of the dirty old man as someone who can be picked out of a crowd must be discarded. Any man - young or old, handsome or disfigured, strange or familiar - may be eyeing you as his next victim. This doesn't mean all men are sexual predators, but you must always be cautious. People you'd even consider "good guys" or "normal men" aren't always who they seem. They may have deep-seated problems you don't see, which could make them do harmful things to you.

You must understand that such men:

▶ are often known by you;

▶ often seem kind, nice, polite and friendly on the surface;

▶ work at all kinds of jobs;

▶ can be well dressed and look respectable;

▶ can be good-looking or handsome;

▶ are generally suspected by no one.

Some of the things you can do to protect yourself from such people include:

▶ be attentive;

▶ be alert;

▶ be guarded in your relationships with strangers, even on dates;

▶ have well thought-out strategies to deal with difficult situations;

▶ trust your instincts.

What else could you do?

_____

_____

_____

_____

_____

_____

_____

_____

_____

_____

_____

_____

_____

_____

_____

_____

_____

_____

_____

_____

_____

_____

_____

"Always, always be aware!"

An exhibitionist is exposing himself to you and your friends.

The Exhibitionist

There are some men who feel the uncontrollable urge to expose their sexual organs in public. Most of them bare themselves in front of girls and women. Some also touch themselves in the process.

The girls or women generally become shocked or upset; they stare at the man (which is what he wants) or they run away screaming.

Certainly, exhibitionists are in need of help, but they're usually not violent. It's enough for them to expose themselves to you and they often do so without becoming violent. Therefore, you have no reason to panic!

What do you do?

▸ Walk away without paying too much attention to him.

▸ Report the man to the police and to your parents.

▸ Provide a description of the person which is as realistic and accurate as possible.

What else could you do?

Guys Who Sexually Harass Girls

Unfortunately, not all sexual intruders in your life are as non-violent as the exhibitionist. You now know that the typical "evil stranger" isn't the only person who poses a danger. Most victims know their offender.

How can you protect yourself against such people? In the chapter entitled "Protecting Your Boundaries," we divided various types of behaviour into categories: Nice, Okay, Don't know, Stupid and Disgusting (see page 88). Now you know what kind of treatment and touching you find acceptable and where you draw the line. Remember to always stand firmly by your decisions. Don't be pressured into doing something you feel is wrong or inappropriate. You have the right to say NO!

Learn to distinguish between those who respect you for who you are and those who wish to manipulate or control you for their own selfish desires. In the remainder of this chapter and the following chapter, we'll examine scenarios of sexual aggression, tips for prevention and how to respond when things threaten to get out of hand.

The Challenge of Dating

It's never simple to say NO; but if you do say NO, life sure is simpler if you stick to it. Boys will use all sorts of ploys to talk you or even force you into what they want you to do. Be prepared! Here are some preparatory strategies concerning dating contexts. In the next section, we'll look specifically at scenarios of violence. Remember always to develop a strategy - having a plan is smart!

You could:

▸ Have an idea about how you'd like the date to go. For example, after the movie, do you really want to go to his apartment? Would you prefer to go to a café - in other words, a more public environment where you can talk and get to know each other better? Have suggestions ready. Show him you have your own ideas and aren't dependent on his initiative. Exhibit your competence. Research your ideas - call and make sure the particular café or restaurant is still open after the movie or find another one. Arrange to meet friends with your date. Talk to your parents about having some "teen space" in your home with things like music, a pool table, a television or chips and soft drinks. Invite him over. Excite him with your plans. Be interesting and innovative!

▸ Remember that no matter how far you're willing to go sexually, there's always some point where you'll need to draw the line. Don't ever believe you can take the easy way out and avoid ever saying NO. There'll always be some guy or some situation... Learn to say NO! The ability to say NO is a skill you'll need both at school and on a date. Learn to set limits for yourself and others.

▸ If he tells you he's going to die if you don't say yes or that you're responsible for his misery, don't take him seriously! No one ever died from a state of sexual excitement. Further, you're not there to fulfill his every desire. You're an individual with your own needs and desires. Do what is right for you. Strive for a relationship which is mutually rewarding for you and your partner.

What else could you do?

Watch your drink!

Rohypnol and Other Recent Social Realities

Drugs like Rohypnol have always been around, but it's never been more plentiful or easy to obtain as it is today. These drugs are undetectable when slipped into a drink, quickly rendering victims helpless and at the mercy of their partner. Many unsuspecting girls on dates with guys they don't know very well have succumbed to the drugs' effects and the consequences, which too often ends in rape.

Heed the warnings about strangers. It's also crucial to learn to trust your instincts and not to do things or go places with people you don't trust.

Keep this in mind:

▶ don't accept drinks from strangers - buy your own drinks;

▶ don't leave your drink unattended when at a party or gathering;

▶ get a new drink if you leave one unattended while out on the dance floor;

▶ don't accept drinks that aren't in unopened cans or bottles;

▶ arrange to leave with your friends when attending a party, club, bar or social gathering and agree to look out for one another for the duration of the event.

What else could you do?

_____

_____

_____

_____

_____

_____

Although you'd like to trust everyone you meet, it's wise to heed these words of caution: trusting your instincts and listening to your fears is vital to keeping yourself safe. Fear is a warning sign, an alarm that prepares you for what may come next. Don't ignore this natural defense mechanism. Do something to get out of the situation - run, take a dive, strike. Do what you can with what you have at your disposal, but know when to seek further help. And find out who your true friends are before placing your trust in anyone. Above all, trust yourself.

"No one can make you feel inferior without your consent."

-Eleanor Roosevelt

SEXUAL AGGRESSION AND SEXUAL ASSAULT

Sexual Assault

"Sexual assault or the threat of sexual assault is against the law... It can include forcing you to have sex when you don't want to or making you do sexual acts that you don't like. You may agree to have sex because you're afraid. You may agree to have sex when you don't want to because you're in a relationship. This is still sexual assault."[3] When a date or sexual encounter goes beyond voluntary consent to involve the use of force and coercion, either date rape or sexual assault occurs. Offenders are often bigger and stronger than their chosen victims, but these "victims" aren't necessarily helpless. You can avoid becoming the next victim with the knowledge and power of self-defense.

This chapter provides a variety of techniques to use in response to various attacks you may encounter one day. For each attack, there are a variety of possible responses and with practice, the appropriate one(s) will automatically come to mind when needed.

A forceful NO with strong eye contact and a powerful expression is a good place to begin. If this doesn't keep your attacker at bay, a powerful knee kick to the groin will certainly get your message across. There'll always be an opportunity at some point to deliver a strong knee kick to the groin; a punch to the solar plexus, ribs or groin; a palm heel strike to the tip of the nose; a knife hand strike to the side of the neck; or a thumb thrust into the throat. Whatever technique you choose, respond assertively and with conviction. Give it to him with everything you've got! Don't hold back!

It's more important than ever that girls have knowledge of self-defense to give them the confidence to handle themselves in every facet of life - from going out on a date, to walking down the street alone, to giving a presentation at school.

Keep it Simple

Even in a difficult situation, your response can be quite straightforward. Notice that very little could come out of this situation for the attacker. He would have to take his hands away to remove your clothes, to loosen his belt, to open his pants and so on. He would also need to move his legs. Each of these actions provides you with a window of opportunity to strike him while your hands are free and his guard is down. A back-fist to the face, a punch to the solar plexus, a knife hand to the neck, a thumb into the throat, taking his ear or hair off or a knee thrust into the groin - any one of these techniques would be effective.

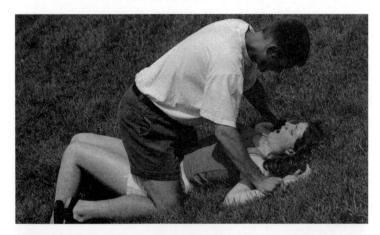

Twist your hip to the right and...

...knee your attacker in the groin. It takes practice, but it's not difficult to do.

NO Means NO

Sometimes when you say NO, it must be backed up. What do you do when a guy isn't simply "coming on" to you? He won't let you go, even when you strongly said: "Please remove your arm!" Notice the order of events below - first you ask him to let go. If he doesn't, then you strike his ribs. This momentarily "freezes" him. In that moment, you twist his palm up and bring him down into the submission hold. An elbow strike to the ribs can also work on its own. Then, immediately get out of there. It's good to know the submission technique as well; however, it must be rigorously practiced to be effective.

First, grab his right hand with your right hand to keep his arm from blocking.

Bring your left arm across your body (palm up) ready to strike...

into his ribs.

Next, lift his arm up over your head...

and bring it down, twisting his wrist up as you prepare your downward left arm attack.

Push down on his elbow joint with your left forearm. This is an effective submission technique, forcing him down to the ground.

Place his hand on your upper thigh for leverage as you apply intense downward pressure. His elbow is close to being broken.

When he gives up, you can let him go. He'll give up because of the pain and the helpless position of knowing his elbow joint can be broken at any moment. The tables have now turned and he's at your mercy. This type of submission technique is called "killing the spirit."

Getting Pulled Away

This guy is grabbing your arm and trying to pull you away. You may seem helpless with your arm in his grasp, but with self-defense training, the response is easy.

Since there's some distance between you and your attacker (as he pulls you), strike him in the groin with your instep instead of your knee. Look directly at him and hit him right on target.

You could also hit his knee or shin. This alternative may be more effective if his groin is well protected by his legs or if the angle of attack is limited.

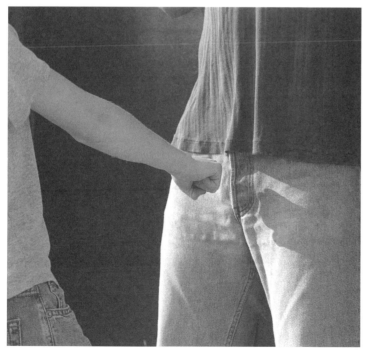

If your hands are free in a confrontation with an attacker, you may also punch him in the groin, use a knife hand to the neck or a palm heel strike to the chin.

113

Raking the Eyes

You can rake your attacker's eyes with your fingers. However, you shouldn't have to use such drastic techniques - not when you have such effective techniques as those described above, which don't result in serious or permanent injury.

Poke your fingers into your attacker's eyes if you have no other options.

Don't Get Carried Away

The attacker isn't just pulling you; he's trying to carry you away! This is much more difficult to handle.

But even as you're caught within his grasp, lifted off the ground, carried off against your will, your legs are dangling in the air, close to his groin, where it would be easy to smash your knee or an instep right between his legs. In fact, it would also be easy to kick his knee or shin. But let's do something different. How about an elbow to the head? After all, your elbow is right there, perfectly positioned for fighting in close.

Your attacker is trying to carry you away.

You can give him a knee kick
in the groin or...

bring your elbow up and elbow him to the side of the head.

Then, knee him to the groin and...

immediately stomp down with a kick to the instep.

Remember: any one technique is enough, but always be prepared for more. If you don't panic, the response is always at hand - or foot!

The Bear Hug

There are several effective moves you can do when you are grabbed from behind.

You're attacked from behind with a powerful bear hug. Out-muscled and out-sized, you depend on the power of technique and the element of surprise.

Lift your left leg and...

bring it crashing down on your attacker's instep.

Bring out your left arm and...

follow with a rear elbow strike to the solar plexus.

You could also bring your arm back up and...

finish with a hammer fist into the groin.

A Walk in the Park

You are grabbed from the side. What do you do in this situation?

A guy grabs you by the shoulder.

Set up for the elbow strike and...

after hitting him in the ribs...

prepare for a knife hand strike...

into the groin.

The secret is practice, but also use your imagination. When you're walking down the street or sitting on a bench, ask yourself: what if this guy does this; what technique would be most effective and appropriate? Practice visualizing in your mind the various scenarios and your responses to them. Talk about them with your friends, practice and be alert!

*"Almost anything is easier
to get into than to get out of."*

-Agnes Allen

DANGEROUS SITUATIONS

Intelligent Choices

If you're attacked in a secluded area, run to an area where there are other people.

Remember:

▶ run out of the park, not into it;

▶ run out of a wooded area, not into it;

▶ run down the stairs and out of the house, not into it;

▶ run out of the cellar, not down into it.

You could be walking alone in a park...
Keep alert.

These are simple choices you can make that can save your life. Kick and punch the person to gain the opportunity to escape. Then get out!

"You Could be a Model"

One trick often used by men to lure girls into a car is telling girls how beautiful they are - beautiful enough to become a model. Once you take the bait, he explains he's a photographer and needs to take some pictures of you in a more suitable environment. He conveniently has a camera and a car; all you need to do is go with him. You're flattered, and it's hard to let such an offer pass without checking it out. Listen to your instincts. Remember: if it sounds too good to be true, it probably is!

It doesn't often happen that a stranger carries his victim off into his car.

Instead, girls willingly consider getting into the car of strangers. Is this wise?

Hitching a Ride

You have to get home and you need a lift, so you try hitching a ride from a stranger. Aren't you putting yourself in a dangerous situation that could be avoided? Don't allow him to get you into a vulnerable position - don't get into the car! Think about alternatives for transportation that might be less risky. When prevention and avoidance aren't possible, the knowledge of self-defense gives you a secondary option. Punch him in the solar plexus, kick him in the shin, knee him in the groin, elbow him to the head....

I'LL BE BACK AT 11:00

Let your parents or someone you trust know where you are and when you expect to be back.

Accept a ride only with a person you know well.

The Front Choke

In a front choke situation, you have two choices: panic and do what he wishes or fight back using the element of speed and surprise.

Your attacker is choking you from the front.

It takes only a split second to forcefully punch him in the solar plexus.

The Rear Choke

When you don't have a clear view of the situation as you would if it were a front choke, it's essential that you deliver two solid thrusts to the attacker.

An elbow strike is ideal for defending against the rear choke attack.

Bring your left hand to your hip with the palm up as if you were going to punch him with your left hand. At the same time, bring your right arm straight out with the palm down.

It's the right hand that strikes as you thrust straight back, jamming your elbow into his ribs.

The left arm should simultaneously thrust forward, adding power to your strike and preparing you for the next strike to follow - a left elbow into his solar plexus.

Grab From Behind

In a situation when you are grabbed and pushed down from behind there are several effective moves you can execute.

Suppose your attacker grabs you from behind by the neck or shoulders and pushes you down. Position your hands in front of you in case you fall forward.

At the same time, lift your right leg in preparation for a kick.

Look behind you to see your target.

Thrust the heel of your foot into his groin.

You're now looking forward because you're being pushed off balance. Pull your kick back quickly and balance yourself with both feet on the ground.

Forced up the Stairs

You're being forced up the stairs. A back kick is an easy and effective defense. If he attempts to push you down, this actually makes the kick easier to execute. If you fall on your back, execute a front kick into the groin.

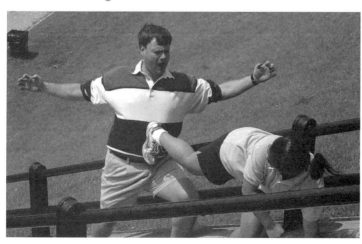

A back kick while forced up the stairs is highly effective.

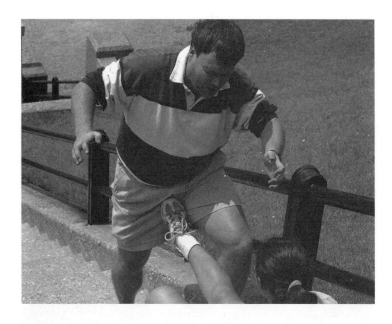

If on your back, use a front kick.

Alone in the Woods

Walking or jogging alone in a wooded area can sometimes be dangerous. Many suspicious individuals hang out there, hidden, where they can remain invisible to the police. The seclusion of the area is ideal for attackers to hide and then attack their victims, sometimes just steps away from "civilization."

When you're jogging out of a dark wooded area in the city, stay alert.

Jogging alone in the woods may not be the smartest idea even if the area is considered safe.

In the Park

In a remote corner of the park, you help your younger brother in trouble. How can you help him?

Punch the attacker in the kidneys.

You can also side kick the attacker in the back of the knee or...

deliver a front kick to the kidneys.

Three-Person Attack

Sometimes you can really be challenged. Walking out of the woods, three guys follow you, moving in closer. Two guys grab hold of you while the third attempts to assault you. It's a scary situation, but you know what to do. First, always go for the guy not holding you - he's the most dangerous one since you don't know what he'll do and his hands are free. The other two are more predictable - their task is holding you. Therefore, when he gets close enough, execute a perfectly timed front kick to the solar plexus. Lift your knee high in preparation for the kick.

After dealing with your most dangerous opponent, you now take on the guy to your right with a side kick and the guy to your left with the same technique . You may decide to kick the middle area of the body (solar plexus or ribs), but it would be equally effective and easier to kick lower - to the groin, shin or knee. You could also use a front kick instead of a side kick by slightly turning your body towards the attacker. Use the technique that's easiest or most comfortable for you.

"Be smart, there's a way out."

Being attacked by three guys is one of the most challenging situations to deal with.

In preparation for the kick lift the knee high...

then deliver a front kick into his solar plexus.

Next, deliver a side kick to the guy on your right and...

a side kick to the guy on your left.

Girl Gangs

A gang of girls confronts you. As with other attacks, RUN, if possible.

Remember:

▶ it's always best not to have to fight;

▶ there's no shame in running and reporting it to the police, the school or other relevant authorities;

▶ save the actual fighting for when there's no way out.

We have saved this defense for last because it's a good review of many of the techniques we already discussed.

"... run!!!"

The first attacker grabs and pushes you.

You respond with a front kick to the knee...

and then quickly hit the girl next to you with a back-fist.

Notice how the attention of the other girls is shifting from attacking to observing and helping the girls you just kicked and punched. Don't let your defences down - you're not free yet.

The third attacker comes at you from the rear.
Lift your knee and ...

execute a stomping kick to the attacker's instep.

There are no more attackers. The remaining girls decided to avoid having the same fate befall them. A little self-defense goes a long way!

Of course, many different scenarios are possible. This example just gives you an idea of what could happen and the type of techniques you could use in similar situations.

"When you know better, you do better."

-Maya Angelou

WHERE TO LEARN MORE

Where Do I Go from Here?

It's not enough to have read this book. All of the skills you learned must be practiced, including:

▶ falling drills;

▶ self-defense techniques;

▶ punches and kicks;

▶ gathering ideas;

▶ developing strategies;

▶ role-playing;

▶ saying NO!

As far as the athletic techniques, it's easy to see why you need to practice - you have to learn them. Developing confidence and decisiveness in your actions requires practice and self-reflection. This will help define who you are and how you'll be regarded by others. You can be hesitant, indecisive and easily influenced by others or you can develop the personal power to make your own decisions with conviction. These two ways of being will result in two very different lifestyles. Only you have the power to determine the lifestyle you lead.

This is a book on self-defense and more. Self-defense training helps define the person - whom you want to become and how you can get there. Self-defense training builds bodies and technique. It also builds character.

This book is a beginning. Continue practicing by yourself or with friends. For readers who would like to go further, here are some ideas.

Where Can I Practice?

At School
Schools offer a lot of possibilities to work on various aspects of self-defense. Talk to your teachers about:

▶ doing the falling drills and other techniques in phys. ed. classes;

▶ watching a film about one of the book's themes in a social studies class;

▶ role-playing in English or social studies class;

▶ working for a week on a project: "Self-Assertion and Self-Defense;"

▶ offering a special workshop in self-defense taught by a qualified instructor;

▶ providing obligatory seminars for boys and girls on "Sex Roles in Society;"

▶ starting a self-defense program at the school with a qualified instructor.

At a Community College or Night School
There are many more courses offered at colleges than most people realize. One course increasingly being offered is "Self-Defense for Girls." If no such course exists where you live, get together with some other girls and get one started. Always make sure a qualified and sensitive instructor offers the program.

At a Youth or Community Centre
Ask the director of your local community or youth centre whether they offer a course in self-defense. They often welcome suggestions from young people as to what kind of courses should be offered.

At a Local Sports Club or Sports School
You can learn and practice many falling and self-defense techniques at a martial arts club or school. But remember, martial arts techniques alone aren't enough to protect yourself effectively! You need an instructor who is competent in martial arts and knowledgeable about the issues and concerns of girls and women in today's society.

At Home
Practicing self-defense doesn't have to be limited to formal instruction at schools or clubs. The various aspects of self-defense outlined in this book can be safely practiced in your own home, provided you exercise caution and self-control. If you've enough space to perform the skills and techniques, the proper attire and the necessary equipment (such as mats, carpets, etc.), you are only limited by your imagination. Get your family and friends involved-everyone can benefit. But always remember to make safety your first priority.

At a Martial Arts School
There are many different Asian martial arts originating from different countries. These arts emphasize different aspects of self-defense:

▶ Judo: an Olympic combat sport that develops agility, balance and quick reflexes through falls, throws, fighting, flexibility and coordination;

▶ Aikido: a Japanese martial art based on falls, throws, avoiding attacks and graceful circular movements;

▶ Tae Kwon Do: a Korean form of martial art promoting hitting, kicking, fighting, blocking, dodging and intercepting with bare hands, arms and feet;

▶ Karate: the focus is on developing punches and kicks with the aim to promote focus, patience, character and respect;

▶ Kung-Fu: promotes building of strong mental and physical level of conditioning through various strikes and blocks;

▶ Ju-Jutsu, Tai-Jitsu and Hapkido: teaches falls, hitting, kicking, breaking free, throws and hold techniques;

▶ Tae-Bo: combines muscle toning and cardiovascular conditioning through self-defense exercises and activities.

Don't be misled by the differing descriptions. Some schools of karate, for example, are more different from each other than from other martial arts. What counts isn't the particular art, but the nature of the program and the quality of the instructor.

Steps in Finding a Good Martial Arts School

Ask around. Talk to your friends and family members. Explain what you're looking for in a school and if they know of a good one. You'll be surprised how only a few schools will be mentioned over and over again by different people as being special.

You can also check the Yellow Pages, but don't be impressed by the biggest adds. Call the local university or college to find out what programs it offers. Universities usually have high standards for their instructors, researching them before making a choice.

Now that you've collected the names of a few possible schools, go visit them. Answers to the following questions will help you choose the right martial arts school:

▶ Are classes interesting, intense, challenging, meaningful and dynamic?

▶ Does the instructor demonstrate as well as explain? Is she a good role model capable of maintaining high standards?

▶ Is there a definite female presence in the school? Are there women black belts and instructors? Are the women as good as the men? In a good school, they'll be every bit as excellent!

▶ Are there only or predominantly white belts (beginners)? A good school should have a reasonable distribution of all belts, indicating that the beginners are advancing, rather than dropping out.

▶ Are promotions automatic, according to length of time studied or prepayment for the next level? A truly good school never promises promotions according to any pre-arranged "deal."

Promotion should only be according to the progress of the individual in line with high standards.

▶ Is there a philosophy to the school? Often this is expressed in its brochure. What is it - winning trophies or developing the potential of each student? Are they true to their philosophy in the action of the class?

No matter what you pay for good martial arts training, it's worth it. Yet, avoid schools where you must sign long-term contracts or where they discourage you from watching classes before joining. A truly good school will be reasonable in its fee structure and fair in its treatment of students. The best school isn't necessarily the most expensive.

Martial arts should be fun. Serious, yes; but also fun.

Other Options

Aside from practicing at the various locations mentioned, there are a variety of other means by which you can learn more about self-defense. In an age of increasing technology, various media have made information more accessible than ever. The following sources of information offer further options in your pursuit of self-defense knowledge:

▶ Cable Television, e. g., PBS

▶ Internet Web sites;

▶ Video rentals;

▶ School/Public library books;

▶ School/Public library videos;

▶ Specialty magazines.

By accessing as much information as possible from as many different sources as possible, you'll gain a broad perspective on the subject and open your world up to a wide range of possibilities. It's up to you to find out which sources are the best for you.

WHERE TO GO FOR HELP

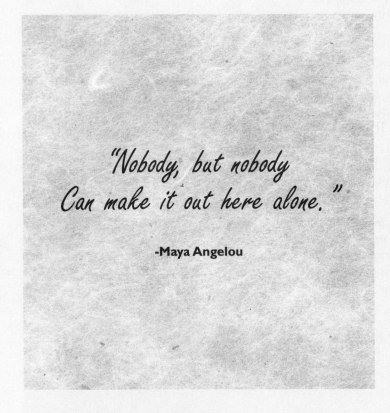

*"Nobody, but nobody
Can make it out here alone."*

-Maya Angelou

There's Help! You're Never Alone!

Sometimes you really do need help from others when there's trouble in your life. Help may be as near as a parent or sibling or someone you trust including friends, teachers, the police or youth services. You shouldn't have to deal with serious incident on your own.

If you need help, self-defense techniques should be your last alternative. Self-defense will help in the crunch, but first look into techniques of avoidance. If there's an existing danger or a continuous situation of abuse or harassment, contact the agency or individuals listed.

Agencies and Individuals Who Will Help You

Your School Principal or Guidance Counsellor

Many schools have resources right in the building to help young people deal with problems. Most schools have strict policies dealing with sexual abuse or harassment and will take measures to help you deal with the problem.

Youth Services

Many areas will have a youth services office, either private or connected to local government. You'll find help there if you can't get help from your family.

Girls' Shelters

In many cities, there are girls' shelters where young girls and women who have been abused or assaulted can find refuge. If there's no shelter in your area, you may be able to find a women's shelter where you can go for help.

The Police

If you're in danger, the police can help. You can telephone them quickly and ask for assistance. In most telephone booths, you don't even need money to phone. Just dial 911. Keep in mind, however, that the police can't solve all your problems. It's up to you to take the appropriate steps.

What is a Hotline?

Whenever you need a sympathetic ear or somewhere to turn for assistance, hotlines offer an important service. A number of telephone hotlines are available for numerous concerns including assault, sexual assault and various distresses (such as Kids Help Phone).

Many of these calls are toll-free (1-800 or 1-888), making it accessible to most people. Hotlines provide an outlet for you to discuss your problems without being judged or ridiculed, while respecting your anonymity. Having someone listen to your concerns and provide you with information and guidance is vital in a time of need. It's comforting to know others understand what you're going through and are willing to help you get through it.

Emergency Situations

In an emergency requiring immediate protection from physical harm or medical assistance, **dial 911** for police and/or an ambulance.

There's no charge for these emergency calls. Most public telephones are equipped with 911 service and require no money. If 911 service isn't available, **Dial 0** for an operator and explain you need the police or an ambulance or both.

To find other emergency numbers, look under the heading of Emergency Numbers in the telephone book for your area. This information is usually on the inside cover or the first few pages.

You can also try dialing **411** and ask for the type of service you need.

Some services accept collect calls if you can't pay for the call (even if it's a

A number of telephone hotline numbers are available for you to access during an emergency.

local call). Dial 0 plus the area code plus the number. Some numbers begin with 1-800 or 1-888, which means you don't have to pay for these calls and it won't appear on your phone bill.

National Sources for Information and Action

To learn more about violence in youth relationships and for help in dealing with violence or abuse, contact one or more of the organizations listed below.

The United States[1]

National Domestic Violence Hotline
1-800-799-SAFE
Information, support and referral to women's shelters in your area.

National Victim Center, INFOLINK Program
1-800-FYI-CALL
Comprehensive information and referrals to more than 8,000 victim-assistance programs across the United States.

Big Brothers and Big Sisters of America
(215) 567-7000
Information on how to become involved in this time-tested much-honored institution.

Canada[3]

National Clearinghouse on Family Violence
Health Canada
1-800-267-1291
TDD 1-800-561-5643
Room 1108, Finance Building
Postal Locator 0201A2, Tunney's Pasture
Ottawa, ON K1A 1B5

Kids Help Phone
1-800-668-6868
439 University Ave., Suite 300
Toronto, ON M5G 1Y8

White Ribbon Campaign (Men Working to End Violence Against Women)
1-800-328-2228
220 Yonge St.
Galleria Offices, Suite 104
Toronto, ON M5B 2H1

The Body Shop Canada
1-800-387-4592
33 Kern Road
Don Mills, ON M3B 1S9

YWCA of Canada
Community Action on Violence Against Women
(416) 593-9886
80 Gerrard St. East
Toronto, ON M5B 1G6

The Canadian Women's Foundation
(416) 484-8268
214 Merton St., Suite 208
Toronto, ON, M4S 1A6

Battered Women's Support Services
(604) 687-1868
Counselling: (604) 687-1867
Box 1098, Postal Station A
Vancouver, BC V6C 2T1

**Speaking Out Against Violence
Video Collection
National Film Board of Canada**
1-800-267-7710
D-5, P.O. Box 6100, Station A
Montreal, PQ H3C 3H5

Ontario[3]

An excellent source book for women is
the *Guide to Services for Assaulted Women
in Ontario*, published by Community
Information Toronto (CIT). Well written
and organized, it's available in both English
and French. You can contact CIT at
(416) 397-INFO or from outside Toronto
at 1-800-836-3238. The order desk
number is (416) 392-4575.

I know who I can call...

TIPS FOR THE PREVENTION OF VIOLENT CONFRONTATIONS

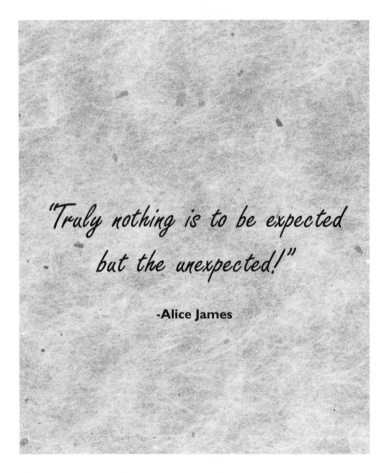

"Truly nothing is to be expected but the unexpected!"

-Alice James

The best way to refuse to be a victim is to have a plan and to portray yourself as a person who refuses to be a victim. The following points will assist you in developing a personal safety strategy.

▶ Don't broadcast your plans in public. Many criminals look for prey using this method of information gathering.

▶ Maintain your personal space. Stay alert! If a person invades your comfort zone, be cautious and move away.

▶ Be alert when leaving any type of shopping facility. Criminals know this is a time when you tend to have a lot of money, cheques and personal items on you.

▶ Don't use bank machines at night or in unfamiliar or unsafe surroundings. These areas are high-risk. With its easy accessibility, criminals find it a profitable target area.

▶ Avoid high-risk areas such as stairwells and isolated washrooms. These areas tend to be poorly lit and under-patrolled by security.

▶ When walking, face oncoming traffic. A person walking with traffic can be followed, forced into a vehicle and abducted more easily than a person walking against traffic.

▶ When being dropped off at a location, ask the driver to wait until you're safely inside. Although this may be embarrassing to you, it can make the difference between being a victim and arriving safely.

▶ If you're in an elevator and someone threatening gets on, get off as soon as possible. If you can't get off the elevator right away, press several buttons for the upcoming floors and get off at the first opportunity. Don't press the stop button. Don't get into an elevator where you'll be alone with a man in what you consider an uncomfortable or threatening situation. Follow your instincts. It will only be a few more seconds to wait for another elevator. Your security is well worth the wait.

- Watch for areas in which lights have burnt out or been removed. Removing, unscrewing or breaking bulbs is a common tactic of criminals. It gives them a comfortable area in which to work, one that you should avoid.
Always be suspicious of such places.

- Carry money outside of your purse. If accosted in a robbery, you can give the criminal "chump change" and still hold onto your personal belongings. Better yet, don't carry a purse at all.

- Before going to bed at night, close and lock your first floor windows. These provide easy entry into your house by an intruder. Don't leave ladders lying around the outside of the house; in other words, don't make it easy for an intruder to enter your house.

- Install dead bolts in your house for added security. Locks are very effective in thwarting the plans of an intruder.

- When away from home, leave lights on so the house doesn't appear vacant and inviting to a burglar. If you arrive home and suspect a burglar is inside, don't enter the house. Go to a neighbour and call the police.

Don't leave your cellular telephone at home if you have one.

- Consider taking a self-defense course. It will be a fun place to meet interesting people and it may save your life. Search for an excellent school that meets your needs and standards.

Bibliography

1. de Becker, G. (1997). *Gift of Fear*, Dell.

2. Insel, P. M. & Roth, W. T. (1994). *Core Concepts in Health* (7th ed.). *Mountain View*, CA: Mayfield.

3. *Guide to Services for Assaulted Women in Ontario.* Community Information Toronto, 1998.

4. Payne, W. A. & Hahn, D. B. (1992). *Understanding Your Health* (3rd ed.). St. Louis: Mosby-Year Book.

5. Schmitt, G. (1992). *Mädchen Lernen Sich zu Wehren.* Sportverlag, Berlin.

6. *Stop Violence Against Women* (1998). Information brochure distributed jointly by the Body Shop, the Canadian Women's Foundation and the YWCA of/du Canada 1998.

ACCOMPANYING NOTES FOR PARENTS AND TEACHERS ON GIRL POWER

Sport Books Publisher

Contents

*"It's very difficult
to live among people
you love and hold
back from offering
them advice."*

-Anne Tyler

The best thing you can do for your teenager is to encourage her to learn self-defense. There are too many stories about parents who waited too long before encouraging their daughters to learn how to defend themselves. Avoid finding yourself in the same situation! It's a step that will bring you peace of mind and teach your daughter important life skills beyond the physical aspects of training. She'll build confidence, self-discipline, concentration and other skills that will serve her for the rest of her life.

Why Self-defense for Teens?

Teens are increasingly exposed to various forms of violence:

▶ Fights among gangs at school;

▶ Robberies and extortion;

▶ Sexual harassment by schoolmates or even teachers and respected professionals;

▶ Sexual assaults by dates, friends, relatives, neighbours, coaches...

Sometimes parents find it easier not to talk about these issues or to quickly dismiss them after cursory discussion. After all, it's difficult to explain why these things happen or what we should do about them. We don't like thinking about a world which seems increasingly out of control, threatening to drag our children into situations increasingly beyond our control. If only we could keep our teens in the house. It would be better that way!

Of course, it's unrealistic to think we could keep our children in the house at all times. Kids today have more freedom and are more willing to confront their parents. This makes parenting more challenging, but no one said being a parent was an easy task.

Issues of violence in society need to be confronted and your actions are an important part of the solution. It's particularly difficult to get kids to listen and learn these days, but as parents you still have an obligation to provide structure and direction in your children's lives. Their appreciation will come later when they have become responsible adults capable of living on their own, knowing you helped them on that path. First, help them get there. This is where self-defense comes in.

The Problem of What?

It's not just a question of violence against girls in our society, but the role of girls and women in our culture:

▶ to be themselves and not just sexual objects;

▶ to be respected as competent persons, not just "teens" or "girls;"

▶ to have the right to define personal borders and to defend these borders, if necessary.

This book starts with these premises and builds upon the value of respecting the integrity of girls.

Where Does Sexual Violence Start?

Violence has many faces. When power is abused in the violation of personal borders, this is violence. There are many examples:

▶ teachers, coaches and group leaders who abuse special positions in a girl's life;

▶ teachers who manipulate the power of grades over a girl's life and future;

▶ doctors, ministers, social workers, psychologists and others who abuse positions of respect and authority;

▶ relatives who manipulate love which is already present;

▶ boys and men who make sleazy comments;

▶ dates who use the power of friendship to coerce girls into having sex;

▶ boys and men who use the power of alcohol or drugs to get girls to do things they wouldn't do otherwise.

Girls have the right to determine their own personal borders and to defend these borders, if necessary!

Defending these borders can sometimes lead to conflicts because the offenders, their colleagues or even the girl's family may not consider the violations inappropriate. After all, they're just ordinary guys doing what guys do. "Boys will be boys," as the saying goes. Too often, the girl is blamed - "you shouldn't have worn that perfume," "your clothes are too provocative," "you wear too much makeup" - while the parents of the boy will defend his actions to the end of time.

As parents, we need to be more attentive to raising boys who are more sympathetic and respectful towards all others and girls who are more confident and assertive in expressing themselves. Good crime prevention begins here, since girls who know what they want and are able to express it are less prone to harassment. Girls who know how to defend themselves and can fight for their dignity are less likely to be raped.

What Can We Do as Parents?

It's never too late! This book will help give your daughter the power to be herself, to define personal borders and to demand respect. If an assault occurs, call the police, sue the aggressor, visit a psychologist, take all sorts of steps... but this is after the damage has already been done. You can help your daughter(s) by encouraging her to avoid dangerous situations and, if she should find herself in the midst of a conflict, be able to competently defend herself.

Tips for Parents

▶ Read this book with your daughter today!

▶ Practice with your daughter.

▶ Make it fun! This is an opportunity to participate in a meaningful activity with your child. Enjoy it and do everything to make it enjoyable for her. Investing your time now is an investment in your daughter's future.

▶ If you're interested, try to find a good self-defense program or martial arts school (see Chapter Ten) and enroll with your daughter.

Learning self-defense will have a life-long impact. As teens, girls face tremendous challenges: school fights, sexual harassment, peer pressure, date rape, sexual assault and puberty in general. It's not simply strangers with whom we need to concern ourselves. The greatest dangers often come from those we know.

The knowledge of self-defense gives teens the tools to defend themselves against rape, sexual assault, harassment, fights and other confrontations. Yet, the primary lesson of self-defense isn't violence. First and foremost, self-defense teaches prevention: avoiding potentially dangerous situations, listening to your instincts, knowing where to draw the line, knowing how to say NO and how to back it up when necessary. The confidence developed as a result of self-defense training touches every aspect of a teen's life.

As parents of young children, we teach our kids to say NO to strangers. We supervise them at every step. We don't leave them alone in the park or let them cross the street alone. But all that changes when they become teenagers - they inevitably strive for independence.

"I hope we taught her or him well" is a concern of every parent. Do they have the self-confidence to say NO to peer pressure when everyone else is drinking, taking drugs or piling into the car of a 16-year-old at one o'clock in the morning after a wild party? Do they have the skills necessary to say NO to an aggressive and/or persuasive date? Do they have the basic physical skills to back up that NO when they're alone or cornered in a car, apartment or secluded park?

When your teenager finds herself in a difficult predicament, knowledge of self-defense will give her the know-how and confidence necessary to regain control of the situation. The more knowledge and practice she has, the greater the odds fall in her favour. Intelligence is power!

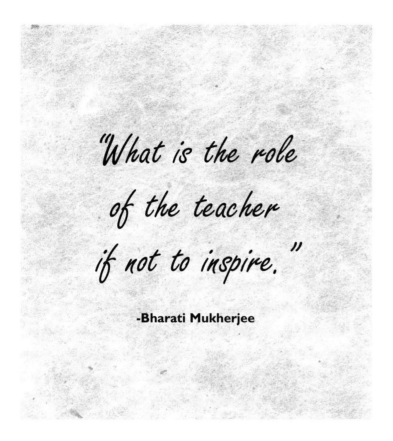

"What is the role of the teacher if not to inspire."

-Bharati Mukherjee

What Can We Do As Teachers?

One of the great joys of teaching is to see a student's life change as a result of the knowledge acquired from our efforts. This short chapter is about being a part of the solution to the problem of violence against girls. It's about teaching girls to be strong enough to defeat any aggressor and to overcome personal challenges that arise as a normal part of being a teenager today.

Self-defense is usually thought of in a physical sense: learn certain techniques and if someone attacks you, let him have it!

In reality, self-defense is a series of life skills encompassing the development of the mind and character of the individual, as well as physical and technical skills. For the teenage girl, studying self-defense means learning how to confront any life situation she faces with confidence: job interviews, math tests, boys who harass her, psychological pressures of growing up and physical confrontations. It means having the character and strength to successfully confront these challenges, as well as specific physical and psychological skills to deal with them.

For teenagers in particular, self-defense training brings a sense of self-discipline and focus to their lives. Studying self-defense and/or martial arts helps them discover their inner strengths, helps them develop confidence in themselves and their skills, helps build their bodies and teaches them how to defend themselves.

Having these skills helps diminish the fear of growing up in an increasingly unpredictable world. They become better students and better people. They would also appreciate support in the development of these important life skills, whether it comes in the form of providing supervised practice time in a gymnasium or developing a program of instruction to supplement the lessons in this book.

National Sources for Information and Action

To learn more about violence in youth relationships and for help in dealing with violence or abuse, contact one or more of the organizations listed below.

The United States[1]

National Domestic Violence Hotline
1-800-799-SAFE
Information, support and referral to women's shelters in your area.

National Victim Center, INFOLINK Program
1-800-FYI-CALL
Comprehensive information and referrals to more than 8,000 victim-assistance programs across the United States.

Big Brothers and Big Sisters of America
(215) 567-7000
Information on how to become involved in this time-tested much-honored institutions.

Canada[3]

National Clearinghouse on Family Violence
Health Canada
1-800-267-1291
TDD 1-800-561-5643
Room 1108, Finance Building
Postal Locator 0201A2, Tunney's Pasture
Ottawa, ON K1A 1B5

Kids Help Phone
1-800-668-6868
439 University Ave. Suite 300
Toronto, ON M5G 1Y8

White Ribbon Campaign
(Men Working to End Violence Against Women)
1-800-328-2228
220 Yonge St.
Galleria Offices, Suite 104
Toronto, ON M5B 2H1

The Body Shop Canada
1-800-387-4592
33 Kern Road
Don Mills, ON M3B 1S9

YWCA of Canada
Community Action on Violence Against Women
(416)593-9886
80 Gerrard St. East
Toronto, ON M5B 1G6

The Canadian Women's Foundation
(416)484-8268
214 Merton St., Suite 208
Toronto, ON, M4S 1A6

Speaking Out Against Violence
Video Collection
National Film Board of Canada
1-800-267-7710
D-5, P.O. Box 6100, Station A
Montreal, PQ H3C 3H5

Ontario[3]

An excellent source book for women is the *Guide to Services for Assaulted Women in Ontario*, published by Community Information Toronto (CIT). Well-written and well-organized, it's available in both English and French. You can contact CIT at (416) 397-INFO or from outside Toronto at 1-800-836-3238.
The order desk number is (416) 392-4575.